Second Edition

Every
Child
Can
Learn

Marie L. Greenwood

With illustrations by
Irvin Wheeler and Master K. Kim

Greenwood&
Associates

This book is a treasure. It is important and necessary reading for all teachers and parents. Way before special education and diagnoses, Mrs. Greenwood was touching children in a very special way. She has the innate ability to instill confidence and the joy of learning. In this book, she weaves a tapestry of vignettes demonstrating the fundamental principles of teaching - believing in all children's ability to learn, instilling the importance of a strong foundation in the knowledge process, and knowing the pedagogy that is best for each child. Throughout, she shows us the power of high expectations, firmness with love and a caring spirit.

Thank you Mrs. Greenwood for being, thank you for sharing your wisdom. You are an inspiration to us all.

Gayle Banks Hamlett, MEd. Psy.D.
Psychologist and Educator

I must say that I thoroughly enjoyed reviewing EVERY CHILD CAN LEARN! Mrs. Marie L. Greenwood provides an extraordinary example of the most important fundamental factor in a child's education – a caring quality teacher! A multitude of lessons on effective teaching can be gleamed from Mrs. Greenwood's experiences spanning decades with children representing both challenges and opportunities for personal and professional growth for even the most astute educator. EVERY CHILD CAN LEARN transcends our nation's current emphasis on the No Child Left Behind educational policy and speaks directly to often times neglected, but essential characteristics of effective teachers: love for teaching all children regardless of their personal disposition, flexibility and creativity in instruction and classroom management, and a firm belief and commitment to bringing out the highest level of success in each and every child. Without a doubt, Mrs. Greenwood book epitomizes the important role that the attitudes, behaviors, and personality attributes of a teacher serve in the academic and interpersonal growth of children. EVERY CHILD CAN LEARN should be on the required reading list of all current and aspiring teachers!

Dr. Anthony P. Young, Past National President
Association of Black Psychologists

Acknowledgments

Thanks to the persistent encouragement of my son, Bill Greenwood, for inspiring me to write this book and supporting me to the end.

The enthusiasm of my granddaughter who has helped in every way possible, Chrissy Weathersby, has added to my joy of writing.

My sincerest appreciation goes to Valerie Thomas for the time she spent proofreading and making positive suggestions, as well as the many hours spent typing and making necessary copies of this manuscript. Her help as project manager during pre-production has been priceless.

I shall be eternally grateful to Librarian Terry Nelson, Director of Blair-Caldwell African-American Research Library for her professional advice, confidence, enthusiasm and assistance in helping to bring this book to completion.

I remember friends and associates who have told me, so often, that I should write my life story. This is one small phase, one of my greatest rewards.

My sincerest appreciation for the positive, educational analysis written by psychologists Dr. Anthony P. Young and Dr. Gayle Banks-Hamlet.

To Mr. Irvin Wheeler and Master K. Kim for the expressive illustrations that so aptly depict the essence of my stories, thank you; and, to Gary Otte for his photography.

Finally, thanks to two special principals, Lila O'Boyle and Mildred Biddick, and to the teachers, parents and children of the Denver Public Schools who have made these revelations possible.

Foreword

Marie Greenwood, a master elementary school teacher, is sharing with us her passion for education. In this book she talks about how she identifies that special child who needs additional attention to develop the confidence to learn.

From the beginning of her teaching career until her retirement she lived her philosophy that, **"Every Child Can Learn."**

Her tenacious dedication to the educational success of children is warmly retold within the expressive stories in this book. Every person is a teacher.

Charleszine "Terry" Nelson
Senior Special Collection and
Community Resource Manager
Blair–Caldwell African American Research Library
Denver, Colorado

Contents

Acknowledgments   vii

Foreword   ix

Introduction   xiii

The Beginning   1

Little IQ 67   7

Handsome Boy, Clarence   11

Big Girl, Dora   17

Stubborn Mattie   21

Belligerent Marilyn   27

The Transition   35

Chairless Charles   43

Big Ben   57

Tiny Tommy   67

Attentive Betty   71

Brilliant Robby   75

Summary   83

Introduction

"I was elected to the Delta County School Board in November. I had been thinking of running for the School Board for many years and I finally did it…. I am going to have a lot to learn in order to do this job well! As I do my work on the School Board, no doubt I will be applying some of the things you taught me in first grade in 1955."

This is an excerpt from a letter I received from one of my former, very bright, first graders. It emphasizes the importance of giving children the best start possible and early!

The narrations in this book are about a few of the memorable children I had during my thirty years of teaching first grade. The emphasis is on reading. <u>Teach a child to read and you can teach that child anything.</u> However, children with special problems must be dealt with individually.

Although these experiences are about first graders, teachers in other grades may find some thoughtful revelations in the conclusions at the end of each story.

I have been retired for many years, but I am still doing my best to inspire and promote the interest in reading. For twelve years I read stories to Head Start, Pre-school, and Kindergarten children through the Denver Public Library Read Aloud Program.

Now, I go out to my namesake school every two months during the school year and spend all day reading stories to all the grades, first through fifth, at Marie L. Greenwood Elementary School.

THE BEGINNING

It was early June, 1935, and the week before I had just graduated with a degree in Kindergarten-Primary Education from Colorado State College of Education in Greeley (now University of Northern Colorado). I should have been elated, but I was frustrated, worried and depressed. We had no money, not even enough to buy stationary and 3 cent stamps (postage in the 30's) to send for applications for jobs.

In 1934 Mr. William Parks, a community leader, and Rev. Russell S. Brown, my minister, had urged me to take the test for teaching in the Denver Public Schools. I had earned my Life Certificate to teach in Colorado. In those days, after completing two years of training in a state school of education one automatically received a certificate which qualified that person to teach in Colorado for life. This was a carry-over from early days when teachers needed only two years of training in a "Normal School." However, in one more year I would receive my B.A. and I desperately wanted that degree, so I said, "No."

It was a very difficult decision to make because for the first time in the history of the Denver Public Schools the door was being opened for us minorities to teach. Whittier Elementary School was in the Black community. After years of the community leaders pleading with the School Board to hire teachers of color, the principal of Whittier, Lila O'Boyle, announced that she would be happy to have a colored teacher on her staff. (In those days we were known as Colored or Negro.) Since I had turned down the offer to take the test, an experienced teacher who had taught for years in Oklahoma and Texas, Dorothy Burdine, was hired. She wanted to return to Denver to look after her elderly parents. She was hired as a permanent substitute and was later placed on contract, without success.

With encouragement of Mr. Parks and Rev. Brown, in the spring of 1935 I did take the Denver Public Schools tests, but I held no hope for any possibility of a job. I felt the door had been closed when Dorothy Burdine was hired in 1934.

In my devastated state of mind I began to regret having passed up my opportunity in 1934 and I could see no other outlet. To add to my depression on that day in June, the mail came and there was a letter from the Denver Public Schools. I was afraid to open it because I could not stand facing a letter of rejection. I do not know how long it took me to muster the courage to open this announcement, but eventually I slowly pulled the envelope open and read:

> June 13, 1935
> My Dear Miss Anderson,
>   At the regular meeting of the Board of Education on June 12, 1935, your probational appointment was approved, effective September 1, 1935.
> Yours very truly,
> R.A. Puffer

Enclosed was a pink probation appointment card appointing Miss Marie Louise Anderson to a position as a teacher in the Denver Public Schools for an annual salary of $1200.00 effective from September 1, 1935 to September 1,1936. I was flabbergasted! I let out a yell and began to cry. My mother came rushing from the kitchen to see what had happened to me. I was weeping and told her, "I have a job in the Denver Public Schools!!!"

$100.00 per month was like "manna from heaven" in the middle of the big Depression of the 30's. Of course, I was assigned to Whittier School.

I had vowed that when I got a job I would get my parents out of that dim basement apartment building where they were working so that I could get an education. My father was also a custodian, all day, at the exclusive Daniel and Fisher department store, so my mother did most of the work at the apartments during the day. The hard work was taking a toll on her health and I was determined to see that she would not have to work anymore, unless she wanted to. I found a house to rent and we moved in; my dad and I shared expenses.

I had graduated with an "A" in student teaching, but since I was the "wrong" color, I was not permitted to teach a single day at Colorado State College of Education. I wrote excellent lesson plans and watched others teach from my plans. This extended observation was in the campus training school, a class of 25 kindergarten children with no IQ's under 100 and managed by soft voices and gentle control.

When I reported to Whittier School I found myself with a first grade of 30 children with IQ's of 67 to 110, in a room with rows of old fashioned desks screwed to the floor. The soft voice and gentle control did not work in public school!

One day Miss O'Boyle came into my room and the noise almost blew her out the door.

"Miss Anderson," she said, "I want to see you after school."

My only thought was, "There goes my job!"

When I stopped in the office after school, all Miss O'Boyle said was, "Miss Anderson, you have to get control. Don't worry about teaching. Get control and then you can teach."

I told her what my experiences were in college and the only method I knew was the theory of a soft voice and gentle control.

Miss O'Boyle looked me straight in the face and said, "Forget the theory!!! Do whatever it takes to get control!"

"Whatever it takes?" I asked in amazement.

"Yes, whatever it takes, get control," she answered. "And bring the tone of your voice down."

I didn't realize, in my frustration, that my voice had reached a high pitch.

That was on Friday, so I had the weekend to develop a plan. I had two goals. I had to keep my job in the middle of the Depression and I had to keep the door open for the others to come in. (No others of our race were hired until I made permanent tenure in 1938.) Since Miss O'Boyle had emphasized, "Whatever it takes," I remembered some of the methods my mother had used to discipline me.

Needless to say, come Monday, Miss Anderson was a changed person—no more soft, high-pitched voice. I was one positive teacher who made it very clear that work would be done quietly; attention was expected from all or there would be serious penalties for any misbehavior.

I had control and I began to teach---the joy of my life!!! These are the stories about my experiences in teaching a few of my Very Special children.

LITTLE IQ 67

This little boy, with an IQ of 67, had just about worn me out. I was at my wits end with him. He was completely undisciplined. Little IQ 67 would get up and walk around, climb up on the desk and make strange noises. He did not talk, and seemed not to understand anything said to him.

When I finally got control of my class, I knew something had to be done to keep him from causing a disturbance so I "zeroed in" on him when he got up to move around. I grabbed this little fellow and plunked him back into his seat. (In those days "laying on of hands" was permissible.) I told him, "You are to stay in your seat!"

He looked at me in surprise with big, wide eyes. Every time he got up, I was on him again. Eventually, he got the message and wiggled around in his seat, but he did not get up.

Then I began to wonder what could I do with this child. Could I teach him anything? He had no idea of how to hold a pencil. When I gave him a picture to color, he would take the crayon in his fist and wildly scribble all over the paper.

Now I was enjoying teaching my class, so I wondered if I could get him to learn one thing at a time.

I took a page from a picture book with big, simple pictures. I put a red crayon in the hand of little IQ67, took his hand in mine and very slowly, carefully, began to outline the picture. Then we slowly colored the picture within the outline. All the time, I was telling him what we were doing. His hand did nothing, since his coordination was so poor. This went on for several trials, until one day I felt his hand working with mine. I let him do the outline, slowly, by himself and praised him for it. He wiggled and grinned and continued to concentrate on coloring. He did not follow the line perfectly nor stay completely within the outline, but he was trying.

Next, I told him the color of the crayon was red. I coaxed him to say, "red." After several tries he said, "R-E-D." After much repetition, eventually he could tell me the color "red" when I asked him the color of the crayon. This took many days.

I went through the same procedure with the blue crayon. He learned to say, "blue." As time went on, he finally could say "red" for the red crayon and "blue" for the blue crayon. It was amazing how hard he worked and concentrated on outlining and coloring his pictures.

I doubt that he could have associated the colors, red and blue, with anything else, other than the two crayons; but for him this was quite an achievement. I do not know how much more I could have taught little IQ67. THEY MOVED!

From this experience, I learned a valuable lesson. The bit of progress made with little IQ67 convinced me that, given time and patience, EVERY CHILD CAN LEARN -SOMETHING!!!

HANDSOME BOY,
CLARENCE

When I started teaching at Whittier, the community was thrilled to finally have two black teachers, but some of the "elite" society did not want their children taught by a "colored" teacher. Most of the "elite" were those with lighter skin.

The Lorders were part of this select group. "Pappy" Lorders was my barber, one of the best, and I liked the way he cut my hair. His wife, "Madam," had a beauty shop in the back. They were located right across the street from Whittier School.

One day when I went in for a haircut, Pappy said, "Madam wants to see you before you go." I couldn't figure out why, since I was not a member of the social group. However, I was friendly with everyone, and I would occasionally stick my head into the beauty shop to say "Hi" to Madam.

On this day, when I went into the shop, Madam said, "I am so glad to see you, Miss Anderson. I have been hearing about the good things you are doing with the children at Whittier. My little grandson, Clarence, is in first grade at Columbine, but he isn't learning anything." That didn't make any sense, because school had been in session for many weeks. Actually I did not know they had a grandson.

"Have you talked with his teachers?" I asked.

"Yes", she said, "But all they tell me is how cute he is; that he has such a charming personality; and that he is such a darling little boy. When I ask him what he does at school, he just says, 'Nothing'."

"How did you get him into Columbine?" I wanted to know.

"We used a friend's address because we wanted him in a better environment than at Whittier," was her answer.

In those days, Columbine Elementary School was in a white neighborhood with a sprinkling of little brown faces. (Today, it is almost all brown.) Although, Clarence was not brown, he was still classified as "colored." I immediately thought - discrimination!

Madam continued, "Since people are talking about how you are helping children at Whittier, I wondered if you would be willing to take my grandson?"

This was the surprise of my life! It also gave me a warm feeling to know that I really was making a difference in the community.

"Check with Miss O'Boyle, "I said. "I will be happy to have him. I will make no promises, but will do my best."

The morning that Madam brought little Clarence to my room, I couldn't believe what I saw. He was the prettiest little boy I had ever laid eyes on, and I could see why the teachers talked about his personality. He was dressed in the most expensive clothes, he had a Buster Brown haircut; his eyes were his striking feature - big, soft brown velvety eyes ringed with long, thick, black lashes.

I welcomed him to our class and Madam left.

I started checking him out to see just how much he really knew. Every time I asked him a question he would open his mouth with "oh-ah," assume the pose of "the thinker" with his hand under his chin and blink those beautiful eyes. The effect was that he was working so hard to think of the answer that never came. I just moved on to other children for answers and each time he would relax with an expression of relief that clearly said, "Whew, I got by with that again!" He had learned to get by on his charms, but had learned nothing academically.

The first day, I let him get by because I wanted him to get comfortable in my class and to see what the other children were doing.

The second day in reading class when he went into his "pose" I said, "You are a handsome little boy and you know it, but I will not think of you as handsome until you get your work done. Now, we will have no more posing because you really are not thinking. Instead, you are going to pay attention and listen so you will learn how to read." The "pose" had become such a habit with him that he would unconsciously assume it, but every time that he posed, I would look at him, shake my head and say, "Uh-uh."

He began to pay attention, listen and think so he could answer my questions like the other children. He concentrated on reading and learned so fast that his face just beamed with satisfaction. His enthusiasm carried over into everything I was teaching. One day I told him, " Now that you are a getting your work done, Clarence, I think you are a handsome little boy and I am proud of you." He gave me a happy grin and his eyes just sparkled.

Weeks later, when I went for my haircut, Pappy said, "Madam wants you to stop by."

When I walked into the shop Madam exploded with, "What have you done to my grandson?!!"

I couldn't believe it! "What's the problem?" I wanted to know.

14

"There's no problem; he's just wearing me out!" was Madam's reply. "He tells me all about his papers that he brings home. He wants to read to me and wants me to read to him. He counts and writes numbers. He practices writing his name and wants me to help him write. When I'm driving down the street he reads the signs, the billboards and anything else that he sees."

"How does he do that?" I asked in amazement.

"He sounds out the word or asks me what it is if he can't figure it out," she answered. "He talks about Miss Anderson all the time and can hardly wait to get to school every morning."

"I am so glad that what Clarence is learning carries over. He is a bright little boy and I am proud of him." I replied.

With the pride of a grandmother, Madam beamed, "Thank you so much for what you have done for my grandson."

Here was a boy with a keen little mind that could have been wasted; he was well on his way to developing a false concept of the ease of getting by in life on his charms and good looks. Why did the teachers at Columbine let him get away with this pretense?

BIG GIRL, DORA

School had been underway for quite some time when Dora was brought to my room. I was amazed at how large she was for first grade. She was nearly seven years old and almost as tall as I am. (Of course, that isn't saying a lot since I am only five feet tall!) She came from somewhere in the South where schools were segregated, which should not have made much difference since all of my children were assorted shades of brown. However, she was shy and the new class seemed to overwhelm her.

I would ask her a question, she would bow her head, look cautiously around the class and she might answer in a soft voice or she might not say anything. From the expression on her face, I got the impression that she had been made fun of or laughed at-probably because of her size. Maybe she had been ridiculed when she made a mistake, so she made very few responses.

Dora could not read or do much of anything that my children were doing. I had to build up her confidence, so I would smile when I talked to her, I would smile whenever I showed her how to do whatever we were working on. Since reading is the most important skill to learn, I worked especially hard in that area with her. Slowly she began to respond, but if she made a mistake she would get that look of failure.

When she responded correctly I would smile and say, " Dora, that's right; I am proud of you!"

When she was wrong I would smile and give her the answer saying, "Don't worry, we all make mistakes sometime; even I make mistakes." This seemed to put her more at ease and my smile seemed to be a kind of catalyst. She started sitting up straighter, really listening and responding more and more. Dora was slowly learning to read, write, talk and do all of the academic work that we were doing. She lost her fear of making mistakes and even smiled back at me. Her progress was remarkable.

Dora never became overtly aggressive but she had developed a quiet self-confidence as she moved on to second grade.

After all these many years, I see Dora occasionally. She still has that quiet confidence and a broad, pleasant smile. It seems that my sincere concern for her and my warm smile helped Dora overcome her shyness, and to believe in herself and to do her best.

STUBBORN MATTIE

Mattie's mother and I were good friends, but I did not know much about her young children. One night at a meeting at her house she asked me if I would stay a while after the meeting. "I want to talk to you about something," she said.

When the meeting was over and the others had gone, she told me that her daughter was in first grade at Ebert School but she was having so much trouble.

"I know she is a slow learner, but she hates school and she hates the teacher. I have to fight with her every day to get her to school," my friend said in desperation.

"What does her teacher say about her?" I asked.

Her reply was, "The teacher says she can't do this and she can't do that, so she can do nothing with her because Mattie refuses to do anything or even try. You are doing so much good with the children at Whittier that I wonder if you would take her."

I had to mull that over for a minute, but she seemed so desperate that I finally said, "OK, I'll be glad to see what I can do. If Miss O'Boyle approves you will have to clear it with her since you are not in Whittier district."

The transfer from Ebert to Whittier was made and I received Mattie. I found that this child had a stubborn streak in her and since the teacher at Ebert had ignored her, she not only believed she couldn't learn, but she had made up her mind that she would not even try.

During the first few days I gave her a chance to adjust; however, when I would talk to her there was no response - just a belligerent look on her face.

In the 30's we taught the old Palmer Method of cursive writing - the printed script had not yet been introduced in the Denver Public Schools. It took some skill for first graders to learn how to write. When I would have the children practicing at the blackboard (old fashion black slate with white chalk for writing), Mattie would just stand at the board and not even pick up the chalk. I would show the children how to make the lines and ovals and everyone would try, except Mattie. I don't know how I discovered she was left-handed but I thought she might be having a problem adjusting her left-hand writing to my right-hand demonstration. I am semi-ambidextrous, so I went over and put the chalk in her little left hand and using my left hand moved her hand to make the strokes. She made no effort to move her hand; it was perfectly limp. It took several days of this procedure before I felt her fingers tighten on the chalk and begin to move with me. All the time I kept talking to her about what we were doing and gradually she began working on her own.

I went through the same procedure with her when we were practicing on paper. She would not pick up her pencil, so I put it in her left hand and we made ovals. One day, I could feel her hand moving with mine so I slowly let go and she continued on her own. "Mattie, you did that all by yourself!" I exclaimed. Soon we began working on writing her name.

The children in the class had been watching, all along, and when one day I announced, "Mattie wrote her name all by herself!" the children clapped and for the first time, Mattie smiled.

At reading time, she said nothing and really paid little attention to what was being taught in this very slow group that was just starting to work on the Scott Forsman pre-primer chart - the Dick and Jane series. Mattie completely ignored the chart we were working on. I would give her a word card (probably see or Jane) and tell her to repeat after me - no response. Day after day, I patiently worked with her until one day she actually repeated the word in a soft voice. "That's good! Now I want you to remember that word so you can tell me when I come back to you. Say it quietly over and over to yourself."

I was elated that she had spoken, and to my surprise, when I came back to her and asked her what the word was, she looked at me and answered. She even grinned! I felt that I had finally broken through the barrier Mattie had built up around herself!!!

The next procedure was to have her get up, go to the chart and match the word card with the word on the chart, like the other children were doing. Just getting up out of her seat seemed to be an effort. She had to make up her mind to move as she glanced around at the others in the group. "Come on, Mattie," I encouraged. "You can find the same word on the chart that is on your card." Finally, she got up, slowly walked to the chart and matched her card with the correct word. From then on she continued to respond and read the words out loud with a happy expression on her face.

When her reading group was introduced to the first pre-primer, Mattie could actually read; SEE DICK. SEE JANE. RUN, SPOT, RUN.

Along with the words, I was teaching all of my children phonics, **the key that unlocks words.** Slowly, Mattie learned to carefully sound out the simple words as she read. I was so proud of her progress that, when we finished reading the pre-primer, I let her take home a copy of <u>Dick and Jane</u> to read to her mother. She was one thrilled little girl!

Her mother told me Mattie's whole attitude had changed. Instead of fighting with her to go to school, Mattie was up early every morning, before anyone else was up, and wanted to get dressed so she could go to school.

She was absent from school for a day or two with a cold and her mother said she had a terrible time keeping her home. She wanted to get to school because she might miss something. This made me feel that I had achieved my goal with Mattie.

Fortunately, the next semester I had a split 1A-2B class, so I kept Mattie and let her continue to work with my first grade. As she progressed, I moved her into my easy 2B group. By the end of that semester she was ready to move on to 2A with another teacher and she continued the progression through each grade.

Mattie graduated from high school with her younger brother. She is now 70 years old, lives independently in her own apartment, her family and friends keep in close touch with her and I see her all the time at our church, where she is very active. She calls me regularly to keep me informed of her varied activities.

Mattie is one former pupil of whom I am very proud.

It takes understanding and a lot of patience to break down a strong, stubborn resistance, to get a child to open up and to use the maximum of whatever innate abilities that child might have.

BELLIGERENT MARILYN

Marilyn was brought to my room by an older woman whom I presumed was her grandmother. This child was a first-class brat! She talked out loud to the children around her; she seldom finished her assignments; and when spoken to would pout and mumble under her breath.

Sometimes she would get the job done, but most of the time she was defiant and did only what she wanted to do. A few times she answered me with a sullen "No" or "I don't have to." These open refusals pushed my patience to the limit.

I knew she was an intelligent little girl who was missing out on learning because of her defiance of authority.

One day, when I told Marilyn, emphatically, that she had to get her work done or stay after school, she looked at me and said, "You can't make me!" That did it!!! I grabbed that little girl, pulled her out of her seat and headed for the back door of my room. As I opened the door, I said to the class, "This is between Marilyn and me and I don't want to hear one sound from any of you." I closed the door and we were in a small alcove where the children's coats were hung. I shook that little girl and she began to cry. "You can cry all you want, but no one is going to talk to me like that!" I quietly exclaimed. From now on, you are going to get your work done like all the other children or there will be real trouble." (Today, I probably would have lost my job for this, but in the 30's it was accepted.) Marilyn wiped away her tears; we went back into a very quiet room and she settled down to the job at hand.

During the following days Marilyn was a changed child. She came into the room with a smile on her face for the first time! Her reading, arithmetic and everything else improved. She learned quickly and I told her I was proud of her. There was no more defiance. She even got her work done and participated in class with enthusiasm.

Several days had gone by when I saw the elderly lady looking into my room, and then she disappeared into the office. I was busy teaching so I thought nothing of it at the time. Eventually, I saw her leave the office. (The upper half of the classroom doors, in the old schools, were glass like a big window so one could see into the room. My room was across from the office so I could see the comings and goings very well.) In a few minutes, Miss O'Boyle opened my door and said, "Miss Anderson, stop by the office before you leave."

After school, when I went to the office Miss O'Boyle told me that Marilyn's mother came in and she was furious about what I did to her daughter.

"That's her mother?!" I exclaimed. "I saw her come into the office, but I thought she was the grandmother!"

"No, this is an older couple who always wanted a child but never had one until Marilyn came along, late in life. They idolize the child but they have no control over her. They have no idea of what to do with such a young one. The mother has told me that she sasses them and will do nothing to help at home. When they ask her to do small chores, she will tell them, 'No, I won't do it.' She does exactly as she pleases," Miss O'Boyle explained. "However, her mother came in here today under a full head of steam. She was furious about how you had mistreated her child and she was out to get your job!"

I was shocked!!! I explained to Miss O'Boyle exactly what I had done and why I came down on this insolent little girl. "I have had no trouble with Marilyn since I disciplined her. In fact, she has been a happy, cooperative little girl, for the first time since she has been in my room. She is a bright youngster and is finally working hard in school. I have no idea what she told her mother, but I did not harm her. I made it very clear that I expected her to show respect and to get her work done. She has changed so much that I actually enjoy having her in my class."

Miss O'Boyle smiled and said, "Don't worry, I would not let her go to your room, and I sent her home with the assurance that everything would be taken care of."

Weeks later I saw this mother looking into my room and when I looked at her she beckoned for me to come to the door. I thought, "What is it now?" She stepped back when I opened the door and she quietly said," I don't want Marilyn to see me. I don't want her to know I'm here, but I came to thank you for what you have done for my child. She has changed so much at home. She's happy and tells me all about school, but most of all, she wants to help me do things at home. She never did that before, so I just came to let you know how much I appreciate what you have done for her." I was amazed!

I thanked her for letting me know that the change in her daughter had carried over at home. I told her how well Marilyn was doing at school.

To see the change in this child, from defiance of authority to acceptable behavior, was one of my greatest rewards!!!

A belligerent, undisciplined, misbehaving child, quite often, is actually begging for those of us in authority to give them positive guidance and a sense of security.

Whittier Faculty, 1939. I am front row, second right in black dress. Lila O'Boyle, Principal, is top row, far left.

Whittier Elementary School
Courtesy of Denver Public Library Western History Dept.

*My first grade class at Newlon, 1960. Mildred
Biddick, Principal, on right.*

*Newlon Elementary School
Photo taken by: Valerie Thomas*

Greenwood Elementary school, now advanced to K-8
Photo taken by: Gary Otte

THE TRANSITION

In 1943, William R. Greenwood and I were married, and in 1945 I took maternity leave from my teaching at Whittier to have my daughter, Louise. Since my husband and I were both only children, I wanted a family of four children - hopefully two girls and two boys, so at the end of my one-year leave, I resigned and stayed home to have my family. I wanted to give my children what I had been giving other people's children for ten years. I eventually had my four - Louise and three boys, Richard, William Jr., and James.

In 1950 we built our new home on West 6th Ave. in the middle of an oat field, and two blocks away, Newlon Elementary School was being built. The opening of Newlon school was delayed until 1951 because of construction strikes. My daughter entered first grade when the school opened, and I wanted to know if there would be a pre-school for my three-year-old son, Richard. We were the only black family in the school, but the principal, Mildred Biddick, remembered me from my early teaching days and welcomed me warmly. That was a pleasant surprise!

This west Barnum area had been mostly fields with a few houses sprinkled here and there, but with the opening of Newlon School, new homes were being built all over the area. Most of the occupants were families with young children and the school enrollment grew so fast that within two years, first and second grades were on double session.

When I asked about the pre-school, Miss Biddick told me that she had not thought about a pre-school since the school was so new, but with the fast growing number of young families moving into the new houses, there might be enough young children.

"Mrs. Greenwood, if you are willing to be in charge of organizing the pre-school, I will check on possible enrollment and if there are enough children, I will see about getting a pre-school teacher. It will meet only once a week," she told me.

"That will be fine with me," I assured her. "I certainly will do all I can, because I want my three-year-old son to have pre-school experience just as his sister had. It definitely is excellent preparation before entering kindergarten."

There were now enough young, stay-at-home mothers in the Newlon area who were delighted to have their children in pre-school, so I helped get the mothers organized in helping with the children every Friday, along with the professional pre-school teacher. For an hour or more, I would take the mothers to the auditorium, away from the children, to discuss problems, answer questions and exchange ideas. We brought in pertinent information and attended special pre-school sessions together. Over the next two years we got to know each other very well. It made no difference that I was the only brown face in the group, and definitely the oldest and more experienced; we became a closely bonded team of mothers.

When the Newlon P.T.A was organized, I was elected president.

In 1953, when my youngest son, James, was a year old, I decided to return to teaching as a substitute, but only in my favorite levels: kindergarten, first and second grades. I wanted to be free to be at home when my children were ill or needed me. My mother loved to be with her grandchildren, but it was not her responsibility to solve problems when my children needed me. This way, I could gauge my teaching time accordingly.

Louise was in third grade and Richard was in kindergarten at Newlon; little Billy was in pre-school and my mother-in-law enjoyed taking him for me on the Fridays that I would be working. My children were being well cared for, so I was at ease in going back to my teaching.

In all those years, not one African-American teacher in the Denver Public Schools had been placed outside of Northeast Denver - not even to substitute. The excuses given by the Administration were that **we could not adjust to working in an all white school, the teachers would not accept us: and the parents would object.**

When Miss Biddick found out that I was substituting, she actually asked for me when she needed a substitute in the first grade at Newlon. I was surprised and pleased, since I was so familiar with the school and lived only two blocks away. Since it was double session, I taught reading in a room with another teacher in her class for part of the morning and she taught reading with me in my class for part of the afternoon. We got along just fine; I was accepted as just another substitute.

When I am teaching, no matter what the ethnic make-up of the class might be, those children are MY children. I have control and I get desired response. My first day at Newlon went smoothly.

As time went on, I was called often to Newlon and was told that many of the primary teachers would ask for "Mrs. Greenwood" when they knew they were going to be absent, because they knew their classes would be kept in order.

At one time I had several weeks of back-to-back, rather long assignments in Northeast Denver, so I did not hear from Newlon for a while. I began to think I had been forgotten, until one day when I came in from work my mother said, "You have been called to report to Newlon tomorrow." I was delighted and relieved.

When I walked into the Newlon office that morning the secretary greeted me with, "Mrs. Greenwood, we are so glad to see you. We have been calling, over and over, for you, but could not get you!" this made me feel warm all over to know that I was being recognized for my ability regardless of my color.

I explained to her how busy I had been and how happy I was to be back at Newlon.

In the spring of 1954 I had a Newlon kindergarten for so long that I began to feel that it was my own, and I was treated like part of the faculty - even asked to attend faculty meetings!

One day, in the spring of 1955, as I entered the building, Miss Biddick met me with a wide grin. "Mrs. Greenwood, the P.T.A. mothers have asked me why you do not teach here at Newlon as a regular teacher. They are so impressed with your teaching their children." This topped it all, having the mothers asking for me!

"Now," she continued, "I have a second grade opening coming up this fall and I wonder if you would be interested."

I was so amazed that I hardly knew what to say. "You mean the MOTHERS asked for me?! That is wonderful, but I will have to think about it since I hadn't planned on going back to work regularly. I'm really not too sure I would want second grade permanently; I actually prefer first grade."

"Oh, I also have a double session first grade opening and the teacher says she knows you and would enjoy sharing the room with you." This was another surprise!!!

"I will check with my mother and see if she feels up to coming every day. I will let you know," was my reply.

My mother was delighted to come every day; three-year-old Jimmy would be the only child at home all day.

I let Miss Biddick know that I would like to take the first grade assignment, but I wondered if I would be accepted at my age, since I had been off contract for ten years. She assured me everything would be all right and clued me in on a few helpful pointers to remember in my interview with Mr. Bennett, the superintendent in charge of Elementary Education.

Mr. Bennett welcomed me pleasantly and had my file from my early teaching years. He mentioned that I had an excellent record. Then he asked me if I would be interested in taking an assignment in Northeast Denver. I told him, "No, I will only consider a school close to home like Newlon or Cowell. Otherwise, I will remain a substitute teacher, rather than drive all the way across town every day." He picked up the phone, called Miss Biddick, and my assignment to Newlon School, as of September 1955, was settled just as Miss. Biddick had predicted.

I was the first African-American teacher to be assigned to an all white school in the history of the Denver Public Schools, so every week Mr. Bennett called to see how "Mrs. Greenwood" was getting along and Miss Biddick would tell him, "Mrs. Greenwood is doing just fine. She is one of my best teachers." By spring of 1956, he stopped calling.

The administration got the message that qualified, dedicated teachers come in all colors and can be accepted to teach in any school. I had disproved the discriminating excuses given all of those years. In the fall of 1956 two of the best minority teachers were placed in schools in all white areas and they were praised for their excellent work. The door had been opened for teachers of varying ethnic groups to be placed in schools wherever they were needed.

I was in a unique position as I began teaching at Newlon in 1955 with Louise in fifth grade upstairs, Richard next door in second grade, Billy across the hall in kindergarten and the other grandmother bringing Jimmy to pre-school downstairs.

I told Miss Biddick, "I do not want any of my children placed in my room. I t would not be fair to my child or to me, because I might be too easy or too hard on him in trying not to show favoritism."

I informed the teachers, "Treat my children as you would all the others. You will be doing them no favor letting them get by easy. Whatever your discipline methods might be, use them! At school, I am just another teacher. I become mother when I get home." I also made the same information clear at home.

Several times I was asked to go into administration. No way! I loved teaching first grade and I did not want to deal with anyone over eight years old!

I spent eighteen most enjoyable years at Newlon School before I retired in 1974.

The following stories are about some of the children who made my first grade teaching at Newlon worthwhile.

LETTER from a former student:

August 28, 1993

Dear Ms. Greenwood,

> *I was in the second year of my first grade when I met you. I called you Mrs. Green at that time. Reading was a struggle that I thought I could do without. To this day I can remember the patience and understanding that you displayed.*
>
> *As I finished school, I was told that college was not a good place for me. I accepted this for many years, until my son started having reading problems in the first grade. It was me all over again and he did not have someone special like you.*
>
> *I was determined to help my son. First I needed to go to an adult education class to spruce up my skills, then I attended Eastern Montana College. There I received a BS in Education and majored in Special/Elementary Education with a science emphasis.*
>
> *In between going to college and family life, I tutored my son in school. He is now in 6th grade and still struggles in reading, but he is following my footsteps.*
>
> *As I think back my eyes still tear up when I think of you. And I still get that determined stubborn streak when*

I think of that counselor's advice. I would love to show him my diploma which reads WITH HONORS.

When my mother sent me the article out of the Denver Post, I knew I needed to thank you and give you an update of a past student. Now that I am a first year Resource Room Teacher, I relish the thought of one of my students doing the same thing.

I admire you and thank you for what you have given me. I hope to do the same for my students.

Thank you for being there.

D. G.

Chairless Charles

Charles was a boy who had lived in several foster homes and had been a problem child in three other schools. He was tall for his age and appeared to be a very normal boy-except for a mischievous gleam in his eye.

The first few days of adjustment were not too bad. He liked to whisper to the children around him and I noticed that he occasionally tipped his chair back on two legs because his legs were a bit long for our first grade chairs.

When he didn't finish his unsupervised work, I reminded him that his talking was preventing him from finishing and he was also disturbing the other children. He definitely knew what to do and would go to work for a while.

For several days he showed no overt rebellion which I had expected: until one day his chair hit the floor. Of course, this attracted my attention and the children looked at him. He had a silly grin on his face, picked up the chair, sat down on it and pretended to go to work. A few minutes later the chair hit the floor again. I was busy with a reading group and looked over at him.

"Charles," I said, "You will have to stop tipping your chair back on two legs. A chair needs four legs to stand on." With a smile he went back to work.

Several times during the day, the chair went down; the children were beginning to take it as a big joke and Charles was quietly enjoying the attention.

When he came for reading, he would flip his chair, at least once.

I knew I had to figure out some way to eliminate this disturbance, so the next day when the chair hit the floor, I walked over and quietly picked up the chair, placing it against the wall. Without raising my voice I said, "Since you do not know how to sit on a chair properly with all four legs on the floor, you will have to do your work standing on your own two legs. A chair cannot stand on two legs, so you let me know when you are ready to sit on the chair with all four legs on the floor. Your chair will be right here against the wall."

Since he was no longer amusing the class and getting my attention, he went to work as best he could by leaning over his desk or getting down on his knees to write.

When he came to the reading group, he was fine for a few minutes when habit kicked in; he leaned back and down went the chair. "Well, Charles, since the chair cannot stand on two legs, I guess you will have to just stand on your own two legs," I said as I put this chair over against the wall.

While we were reading Miss Biddick peeked in the door, as she frequently did. She saw Charles standing in the class, so she tiptoed in, picked up the chair and quietly said to him, "I think you need to sit down."

Immediately I spoke up, "Oh, no, Miss Biddick, Charles does not know how to sit on a chair. He thinks it can stand on two legs so it is always disturbing us by falling over. He has to stand on his own two legs until he learns to keep his chair on four legs."

"Oh, excuse me," said Miss Biddick as she put the chair back against the wall and tiptoed out.

After school, when I was in the office checking out, Miss Biddick came over to me and smiled, "I apologize to you, Marie. I thought Charles was pulling a fast one on you."

I laughed and explained to her what was going on.

A few days later Charles raised his hand and announced, "Mrs. Greenwood, I think I can sit on my chair properly."

"OK, Charles, you may have your chair again but if it falls on the floor just one time, I will take it away permanently and you will have to stand on your two feet for the rest of the time you are in this room," I warned him. "So, be sure you keep your chair on all four legs."

With his long legs, every now and then I would see him tip the chair a bit, realize what he was doing and immediately put the chair on all four legs. Eventually, the chair stayed put as he sat on it.

A week or so later, Miss Biddick stopped in again and Charles was sitting in reading class like all the other children. She quietly came over and complimented him. "Yes, Miss Biddick," I smiled, "I am so proud of Charles because he has learned to sit on a chair properly." Charles grinned and his eyes sparkled.

I do not know why Charles had trouble at his other schools. Maybe it was his subtle way of being conniving to get attention. I had very little trouble with him after he realized that he had to pay for his little irritations and I was not upset.

I always praised him for his good work and the things he did right, but I let him know with a quiet, authoritative voice what was unacceptable when he was out of line. He was an average learner.

After the chair incident he seemed to get the message that I would take no foolishness. He liked attention and praise but to get it in my class he had to obey the rules or pay the penalty, so he buckled down to work and earned my complements.

When he left me for second grade, he seemed to be a happy, confident, well-behaved boy with a mischievous twinkle in his eyes.

I have no analysis for Charles' learning to conform. It just seemed to happen!!!

CALMING KATE

I seemed to have become the first grade trouble-shooter because I received practically every first grader who entered Newlon with a questionable problem. This time, Miss Biddick informed me that the child I was to receive had been expelled from a Catholic school first grade after only a few weeks of school.

"She is so unruly that the nuns have given up on her," she explained. "They refuse to let her return to school, and her mother is at her wits end."

"My goodness, she must be really bad for the nuns to give up on her!" I exclaimed. "I have never heard of a child being expelled from a parochial school."

I wondered to myself, "What am I going to do with a child like that?"

We were on double session and I had an afternoon class.

A day or two later, when the little blue-eyed blond girl was brought to my room, I was amazed to see that she was Kate who lived across the street from us and played with my boys and other children in the block! I knew that she went to Catholic school, but she always seemed like a normal, active little girl who enjoyed playing with the boys, since most of the children her age in our neighborhood were boys.

I placed Kate in a front seat so I could keep an eye on her. Right away she began to chatter with the children around her. Even when I was teaching the class her voice could be heard, almost non-stop. When I would speak to her about her talking and disturbing the class, she would turn a bit red, either look down with her mouth set or look at me with a determined expression that implied, "OK, I hear you but it makes no difference to me." As soon as I moved on from her the chatter would resume.

She had devious ways of starting an argument. When getting a retort back from one of the children after she said something to him, up would go her hand, "Johnny called me a name," she would whine. In line, she would push someone or get in ahead so there would be a disturbing reaction.

The gym teacher reported that she was constantly causing problems during their activities with her unending talking or pushing and shoving.

After days of trying everything I could think of, with no effect on her, I came to the conclusion that the only way I would have peace in my room would be to, somehow, isolate Kate. But how?

She still played with my boys, but at home I was mother, not teacher, so all went well.

There was no reason to talk with her mother, because she knew the situation with Kate and was just as frustrated as the nuns had been. Unfortunately, Kate was getting no better at school.

I had a medium size round table in the rear corner of my room and it was seldom used for anything. Underneath was a small enclosed compartment where she could keep her pencil, paper, crayons and other belongings. I could visualize her there, away from the other children but still a part of the class. That could be my only recourse and hopefully it would work.

The next day I was preparing for my class when I heard loud yelling and sounds of scuffling at the outside door near my room. I couldn't imagine what was going on since there was another fifteen minutes or more before school would start. The children were supposed to be arriving out on the playground.

I looked out my door just as Kate's mother appeared with a screaming, fighting Kate in tow. "I'm not going to do it. I hate you!" she yelled, pounding on her mother and trying to break away from her mother's grasp.

"What on earth is going on?" I asked in dismay. I had never seen such a violent rebellion!

"I go through this every day!" said her mother, almost crying. "I have to walk to school with her because she refuses to come alone."

"You mean you have to bring her two blocks to school every day?!" I exclaimed. I thought she was coming to school by herself like most of the other children.

"I'm tired. She's wearing me out, so I told her that I was going to bring her in to see you today. That's why we were having such a fight. She didn't want to come in," explained her mother in tears. "That isn't all. She won't do anything at home. When I tell her to take out the trash or dust or clean up in the house, she refuses. And she treats her baby brother something awful. She hits him, fusses at him and makes him cry. I don't know what to do!"

All this time Kate just stood there, red-faced and displaying a defiant expression. I looked at Kate and said, "I am ashamed of you. Why don't you walk to school by yourself?"

"I'm scared," she whimpered.

"There are other children coming to school. Do they have their mothers with them?"

"No," she replied.

"You play with Billy all the time and he comes to school by himself because his sister and brother come to school at a different time since they are not on double session," I told her. "Unfortunately, you can't come with Billy because he is in the morning first grade, but you see plenty of other boys and girls walking to school at the same time as you. You live only two blocks away. Aren't you as big and brave as Billy and those other children?"

She hung her head and whispered, "Yes."

I spoke to her mother, "Now, you are not going to bring Kate to school any more. She is going to walk to school by herself."

"Kate, you are going to come to school without your mother and when you get here I want you to let me know before you go to the playground. Do you understand?"

Kate nodded her head, "Yes, Mrs. Greenwood."

"Now you go home and I will take care of Kate," I told her mother.

Her mother looked relieved and in a strained voice she said, "Thank you, Mrs. Greenwood."

We had been standing in the doorway of my room all this time, so I took Kate into the room and quietly said to her, "You have been disturbing everyone with your constant talking and not paying attention in class, so I want you to get everything out of your desk and bring it back to this round table. This episode today has been the limit!"

She looked at me in surprise but she didn't say anything.

After she brought her things to the table, I showed her the little compartment in which to put them. "Now, Kate, I am not going to put anyone in your seat." I pointed to the one she just left. "That is your own seat and you may return to it when you learn to control yourself and pay attention to what is going on in class. No more loud talking, no more pushing and shoving and no more complaining. It is strictly up to you as to how long you will have to sit back here at this round table. Do you understand?"

Kate nodded her head, "Yes."

"You are still a part of this class like everyone else," I assured her.

When the children came in and saw Kate some of them asked, "Why is Kate back there?"

"That is between Kate and me, " I told them.

The next day when Kate arrived at school, she burst into the room with, "Mrs. Greenwood, I'm here and I came all by myself!"

"Thank you, Kate," I responded. "I am proud of you." In the 1950's it was safe for children to walk to school.

After the third day, when she came in, I said "Now that you come to school on your own, you don't need to let me know anymore. Just go to the playground and come in with the other children."

At last we had a normal classroom - reasonably quiet, minimal disturbances and few interruptions.

In her semi-isolation, Kate had no one to talk to so she settled down to getting her work done, listening to instructions and answering questions. She began to join in discussions and participate in class activities. Gradually her attitude began to change from defiance and rebellion to cheerful acceptance and cooperation. Kate was a bright little girl and learned quickly.

I was told that she was less disturbing in gym and was actually being helpful.

The surprise of my life came about two weeks after the episode with her mother. I was on playground duty when Kate arrived and came running up to me excitedly. "Mrs. Greenwood," she called out. "My grandma wants to talk to you!"

Immediately I thought, "Oh my, grandma is probably unhappy with me about what I have done to her granddaughter," but I smiled and said, "Fine Kate, where is your grandma?"

She took me by the hand and led me over to an elderly woman standing by the building. "Grandma, this is Mrs. Greenwood," Kate beamed as she looked up at me and her grandma.

To my amazement her grandmother broke into a broad grin, held out her hand and said, "I have been planning to come up to see you for some time, Mrs. Greenwood. You are doing so much for Kate; I told my daughter that I wanted to go to school and shake the hand of the teacher who could tame Kate. She is so much better at home. She actually wants to help and will do what is asked of her without a fight. Oh, sometimes she grumbles a bit, but nothing like before. She is nice to her little brother. Instead of teasing him and making him cry, she plays school with him and makes him happy. I just wanted to shake your hand and thank you. Kate talks about you all the time."

As I held her hand, I answered, "Thank you for coming. You don't know how much this means to me to know that what I am doing here at school is carrying over at home. Kate and I have developed a good relationship with each other and I am proud of her."

I gave Kate a hug and smiled at her as she smiled up at me.

A few days later, Kate raised her hand and when I called on her, to my surprise she said, "Mrs. Greenwood, I think I can control myself now."

"I am so glad to hear that, Kate," I told her. "Now you may move back to your seat, but if you lose control and cause a disturbance again, back to the round table you will go permanently, and you will not have your regular seat anymore. Do you understand?"

"Yes, Mrs. Greenwood," was her answer.

The rest of the time that she was in my room she was a happy, hard-working child. Occasionally I could see that urge to talk out of turn, so I gave her plenty of opportunity to express herself properly in class.

I have seen Kate several times since she is now grown up, married and has children of her own. We always laugh about that first grade experience and she tells me, "The one thing I remember about first grade, Mrs. Greenwood, was sitting at that round table and having to peek around the vase of flowers."

"I don't remember a vase of flowers on that table," I laugh. "But if you remember that so vividly, it must have been there."

"Oh yes, you always had a vase of flowers on that table!" she replies. "I wish my children had a teacher like you."

Kate was smart enough to get the message that her overt actions of getting attention were not upsetting me as she had managed to upset her family and the nuns. During her weeks of isolation she learned that she, alone was responsible for her actions and since it was her behavior that got her into trouble in my class, changing her attitude was the only way to get what she really wanted - acceptable attention.

I shall always remember "Calming Kate" as one of my special teaching achievements.

Thanks to the cooperation of a conscientious family who helped to make the transition possible!

BIG BEN

Ben was a big, happy, husky boy. He enjoyed school and liked playing with the other children, but he had to be careful and not be too rough because he was so big. He was almost a head taller than the other children in my room.

Ben was enthusiastic and worked hard in class, but academically he just wasn't getting it. He was in my slowest reading group, and while the other children gradually learned to read, the words did not register with Ben. However, he never gave up and kept trying.

In math and spelling and all the other basics it was the same. He was so cheerful and tried so hard to remember; I used every method I could think of to help him, but nothing worked.

By March or April I finally began to see a glimmer of hope for Ben. He was beginning to learn a few words in reading and I let him know how pleased I was. However, by this time the class was almost ready to move on to second grade. I could not send Ben on with the class. As big as he was, he still needed another exposure to first grade.

I called his mother and explained the situation to her and assured her that I would be glad to have Ben in my class again in the fall since I understood what he needed.

Ben had arrived late in the lives of his parents and he was their pride and joy. Of course, his mother could not see her son repeating first grade. After much discussion I suggested that she and her husband come to school and observe their son in class.

"Come and spend half a day or all day if you wish," I told her. "However, morning would be best because that's when the basics are taught - reading, math, spelling, and writing."

She checked with her husband and they agreed to visit our class. "Shall we let you know when we are coming?" she asked.

"No, come anytime," I answered.

A few days later they arrived one morning with Ben, who greeted me enthusiastically, "My mom and dad came to visit our school!"

"I am so glad you came." I smiled as I shook their hands and seated them near the reading table.

Ben went through the reading lesson, as usual, happily stumbling on his words while the other children were actually reading.

By this time, so near the end of school, in math, the children had learned the addition and subtraction facts through ten. As we reviewed them, Ben missed every one.

The results were the same in spelling, and his handwriting was very poor. It was quite obvious that he was far behind the rest of the class.

When it was time to take the children to lunch, I told the parents to wait for me, I would be right back.

As I walked back into the room, the parents did not give me a chance to say anything. "Mrs. Greenwood, we have talked it over and we can see that Ben is having trouble," declared his mother. "It will be all right for him to repeat first grade. We can see that he needs it."

"Thank you for coming and observing for yourselves," I said. "I will be glad to have him back in the fall so I can help him."

"Shall we tell him?" his mother asked.

"No, I will tell him. I have my own way of telling children that they need to repeat first grade," I assured her.

A day or two later I had Ben stay for a few minutes after school. I never tell a child during class that he will not be going to second grade. Some other children may hear me and this is just between me and the child involved.

"Ben, you know that you have been having trouble with your work in school, don't you?"

Ben nodded "Yes."

I continued, "Well, the work in second grade is much harder and when you are not ready it can be very difficult. Since you have had so much trouble learning in firstgrade, I don't want you to go to second grade without being prepared. I want you to come back to my first grade in the fall so I can help you be the best second grader. Do you understand?"

Ben looked at me. "Uh-huh," he said.

"Now, since you already know what first grade is about, you can be my helper when the children from kindergarten come to our room next fall. It will be all new to them. They will need help in going to the office, since they have never done that before; and, you can help them learn how we do things our way in first grade," I promised him.

"You will be my special helper."

Ben's face lit up. "I'll be a good helper."

The last few weeks of school closed out on a happy note.

At the beginning of school in September, Ben was the first child to arrive in my room.

"I'm here, Mrs. Greenwood," he gleefully announced.

"All right, I am glad to see my big helper," I replied.

To my amazement, Ben had grown inches over the summer and was now head and shoulders taller than the new first graders! Fortunately, it did not seem to bother him and the smaller children looked up to him and accepted his help.

Of course, the first time it was necessary to make a trip to the office, Ben had the privilege of showing the new Office Monitor the way. When children needed to find something in the room, Ben was the one to show them where it was. He loved being a "helper."

Since he was able to start back at the very beginning with the basics, he began to read. With the second exposure to beginning number concepts, he gained an understanding of math so that he was ready to learn the first grade addition and subtraction facts. This repeat exposure carried over successfully into all of his work. Ben was no "shining light," but by Spring he was up to grade level.

One day Ben came in from the playground absolutely furious. I had never seen him so upset about anything. I was really concerned.

"Ben, what's the matter?"

"Oh, Paul told me I flunked first grade!" he scowled. Paul was in second grade and had been in my first grade the previous year with Ben.

"Well, what did you tell him?" I asked.

Ben looked at me and exploded, "I told him I didn't flunk first grade! Mrs. Greenwood is helping me so I will be the best second grader!" This proved my plan was working.

"Good for you, Ben. You are right. You did not flunk first grade and you are learning so you can be one of the best in second grade. You might be even better than Paul!" I exclaimed. "I am proud of you."

Ben smiled in satisfaction, relaxed and was again his normal, cheerful self.

First grade is the beginning of regular routine, formal education and that is where the early foundation should be laid. I do not approve of "social promotion."

No child ever FAILED my first grade!!! I retained many, but not because of failure. I had them repeat first grade because their academic foundation needed to be strengthened before going on to second grade. With a solid beginning foundation, they could continue to build on it without the constant struggle of trying to "catch up."

Jack and Jill

Jack and Jill were immature twins when they arrived in my first grade. As weeks rolled by, Jack began to adjust and to slowly learn, but Jill would not settle down or even try to conform to our class activities. Gradually her actions became defiant and disruptive.

I called her mother several times, but she did not want to talk to me. I tried to have her come to school for a conference, but she refused.

One day when I was talking to a fourth grade teacher I learned that she had an older brother of the twins in her class.

"The mother came for a conference the other day," said the teacher. "She was concerned about her son's slow progress."

In amazement, I asked, "This mother came for a conference? I have been trying to get her to come for a conference about the twins for months, but she refuses."

The teacher looked at me, then hesitated before speaking again. "Marie, I don't know if I should tell you this, but I think you should know. That mother is prejudiced. She resents having her children in your room. I couldn't believe it when she began ranting and raving about how she hates you because of your color. You should have heard her!"

"Well, thanks for telling me," I replied. "This answers the question of why I cannot communicate with her and why she refuses to come to my room."

A few weeks before school would be out, I called this mother again to let her know that Jill was just maturing to the point of beginning to learn (in spite of her disruptive behavior), and that repeating first grade would help to prepare her for second grade. Jack would be able to go on to second grade.

"No, I do not want the twins separated," she declared. "Jill must stay with her brother."

No matter how much I tried to explain how Jill could be helped, the answer was emphatically. "I want the twins to stay together!"

"If that is your decision, there is nothing I can do about it," I answered. "You will be crippling your child so that she will be limping through the rest of her days in school. The responsibility is yours, not mine, for refusing to permit your daughter to get the help she needs."

In second grade Jill learned very little and continued to be a discipline problem.

Third grade was the same, only worse. By the time she reached fourth grade, she was so impossibly disruptive and had learned so little, that finally her teacher insisted that she be retained. That was really too late!

No one knows whatever happened to Jill because the family did not return to Newlon in the fall. This was an extreme case of maladjustment, but it emphasized the importance of strengthening a child's academic foundation early.

Jill's personality was different from Ben's, so I do not know how much I could have taught her, but I am sure that she would have learned enough to have made her school days much easier and it would have been a far less traumatic experience for everyone.

This was one unfortunate experience which I use to compare the difference between **possible success and unnecessary failure** in school. Laying an academic foundation, as strong as possible, before a child leaves first grade is essential. It is unfortunate that this parent would not cooperate.

TINY TOMMY

Miss Biddick informed me that I would be getting a very shy little boy whose mother was quite worried about him because he was so quiet, talked very little and did not play like other children. They came from somewhere in the South.

When Tommy arrived, I was surprised to see such a tiny, shy six-year old. I welcomed him and introduced him to our class.

"Boys and girls, Tommy is new to our school so we will help him learn how we do the things that we do in our class." We were like one big family and the children were eager to help. They showed him how to get what he needed when he seemed confused and they made sure he had a place in line when going to gym or to lunch. He became their little brother.

At first, he was so quiet I could get very little response from him, so I added a bit of Tender Loving Care along with my teaching. Gradually, he began to come out of his shyness. He started to talk more and to respond in class. It took him a little while to get used to so many children, but little by little he related to them and seemed to enjoy their companionship.

Approximately a week after Tommy's arrival I saw someone at the door looking into our room and then she disappeared. A little while later when we were on our way to gym, we passed a woman standing in the hall near the office. Tommy was just behind me in line and I saw him smile and give a little wave. She waved back, so I presumed it was his mother.

I thought, "I will stop by on my way back and let her know how Tommy is getting along."

She was gone when I returned so I went on to my room.

Later that day when I walked into the office, Jean, the secretary said, "Marie, did you see that woman who was here earlier?"

"Yes, she was standing in the hall when we went to gym. When my new little boy waved to her, I presumed it was his mother."

"Well, she came in here yelling that she wanted her child taken out of your room," Jean continued. "She said her child was so unhappy in your class that she wanted him to have a white teacher. She was screaming so loud that Miss Biddick came out of her office to see what was going on. The mother told Miss Biddick that she did not want her son in the room with a black teacher. She wanted him to have a white teacher."

Out of curiosity I asked, "What did Miss Biddick tell her?"

Jean grinned, "Miss Biddick told her to quiet down and in her usual calm, quiet voice informed the mother that her son would not be transferred from Mrs. Greenwood's class. That Mrs. Greenwood is one of our best teachers."

That compliment made me feel good.

"She also told the mother that she had a choice. She could enroll Tommy in another school, or she could leave him at Newlon, but if he stayed at Newlon he would remain in your room."

"What was the mother's reply?" I wanted to know.

"She didn't say anything. She just left," was the answer.

Of course, Tommy remained in my class. Tommy began to blossom! He seemed happy and started to respond in his quiet way. He was an average learner and seemed proud of his achievements. He would smile and his eyes would light up as he talked. He gradually began to relate to the other children and to interact with them. He was one delightful little boy to have in my class and the children really loved him.

One day, weeks later, Tommy's mother appeared at the door and beckoned to me. I was amazed t see her. To my surprise, she smiled!

"Mrs. Greenwood," she said. "I just had to come and tell you how much I appreciate what you have done for my son. He is so happy. He tells me what he does at school. He talks about the fun he has with the children. He plays with the other children, now. He really likes to read, and he talks about you all the time. Tommy really loves you, Mrs. Greenwood. Thank you so much."

I was happy to know that we had alleviated her worries about her son, but most of all, I was pleased to see her change in attitude.

"We enjoy having Tommy in our class," I assured her. "Thank you for letting us know that we have helped him. He is a charming little boy."

Not only did we phase Tommy out of his shyness and help him to become a better adjusted little boy, but his mother also learned a valuable lesson in TOLERANCE !!

ATTENTIVE BETTY

Betty had been in another school where the teacher had recommended that she be placed in "Special Education" since her learning abilities seemed so limited. Her mother constantly refused, insisting that she remain in a normal class. I have no idea why she decided to enroll Betty in Newlon. Of course, she was placed in my room.

Betty was a sturdy, well-built little girl, but very pale and wore thick-lensed glassed. With her vision problems, I placed her in a seat in front.

She was a very pleasant child and interacted well with the other children. She seemed happy to be in our class and really tried to respond to instructions. Her comprehension was very poor, so I dropped back to simple, beginning presentation of one or two facts at a time with constant repetition. I was amazed at how she slowly began to recognize a few words and gradually began a bit of simple reading. She learned to count to 10 and to recognize many of the numbers on sight.

Betty never caused a disturbance and was always ready to participate in whatever activity we had going. Even with her poor vision she would raise her hand to answer questions, although most of the time her replies were wrong, it did not dampen her enthusiasm for participating. The children or I would give the correct answer and she would cheerfully repeat them, and occasionally, she would remember some of them later, especially, if there had been enough repetition of the same.

Betty wanted, so desperately, to learn that she was always listening; she was always paying attention and concentrating on what was going on. It took me a while to realize how constantly attentive this child was. She was using every ounce of her limited ability and in her eagerness to learn, she was actually over-achieving.

One day I told her, "Betty you are always listening and paying attention so you can learn. I am proud of you." She smiled.

I looked at the class and said, "You are great boys and girls. I wish all of you would pay as much attention as Betty. It would be wonderful!"

When Betty left our class she was reading on a low pre-primer level. She had learned to do a few simple problems by putting dots by the numbers and counting them.

She could express herself vocally, very well, right or wrong. She was no where near grade level, but she had learned more than I had expected and she felt proud of herself.

Her mother was elated with the progress she made, but I don't think she realized that Betty needed special help. Betty's positive attitude and her unshakable determination should have been a catalyst in helping her survive with her limited capabilities.

This was another example that, no matter how much or how little, every child can learn <u>Something</u>!

SCIENCE ♫ Spring Summer Fall Winter MATH $\sqrt{3}$

$\frac{9}{3}$

ART

$2+2=4$

Australia

Spelling

$6 \times 6 = 12$

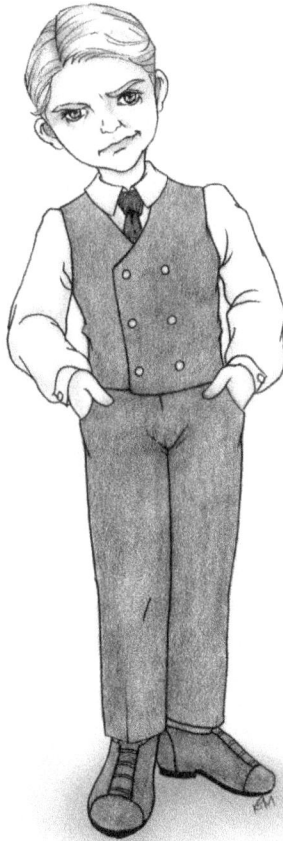

BRILLIANT ROBBY

It was the last day of the school year and teachers were closing up for the summer - there were no children. The kindergarten teacher popped into my room.

"Hey Marie, how are things going?"

"Oh, I'm getting there," I replied. "Are you about to finish?"

"Yes, but I thought I would come over and let you know about a kid you will have next fall. He has just about driven me crazy all year!" she exclaimed. "He constantly told me how to run the kindergarten. He would tell me what to do if I made a mistake. He bossed the children. If they were in the playhouse, he would go in and tell them how wrong they were and rearrange things his way."

"You mean he was only five years old?"

"Yes, so I told Miss Biddick that I thought you were the only one who could probably handle Robby."

"Well, thanks a lot," I remarked. "I'm glad you let me know ahead of time. Let's hope I can handle him." I visualized a big, bully of a boy.

To my surprise, when Robby arrived in the fall he was an attractive little normal-sized first grader with sparkling eyes and a confident attitude. It wasn't long before he interrupted me to "help me" explain what I was presenting. He gave answers almost before I stopped talking. He already knew everything I had to teach a beginning first grade. In my top reading group, that was actually beginning to read, he blurted out answers before the other children had a chance to say anything.

"Robby, you have to raise you hand and take your turn so that everyone has a chance to answer," I told him. He didn't like it but he slowed down.

Within a few days, I realized that Robby was ready for second grade, that he actually knew everything I had to teach to my first grade class - maybe more. He could discuss any subject I brought up in science, social studies or anything else. He could add and subtract while my first graders were still learning beginning number concepts.

Along with all of this knowledge, he had a king-sized EGO! He knew that he knew and as far as he was concerned, everybody else was stupid, including the teacher who seemed to know nothing that he did not already know.

Robby needed more challenge than just my first grade work. I also wanted him to continue working at his level and not just mark time in my room. I told Miss Biddick that I would like to get some second grade reading material for him, in addition to doing my first grade work.

"Check with Elizabeth and see what you can work out," she said. "Let me know how it goes."

I explained to Elizabeth, the second grade teacher next door, and she gave me one of her easy readers and some work sheets to go with it.

Robby could read on that level and do the work sheets, but to let him know that he was still my first grader, he had to do all of our simple work, too.

After a few days, Elizabeth and I decided that Bobby should have the exposure of reading with her second grade class, so he was sent to her room to read with her easy reading group, but he still had to bring his unsupervised work back to our room. He still had to read with my first grade. I did not want to add to his inflated ego by letting him think he was too good for our class. I did not know how I would be able to do it, but that over-sized ego had to be tamed before I would send him into second grade.

Since he already knew all the first grade math, we decided to add second grade math to his schedule. Even though the second grade work and the simple first grade assignments were keeping Robby busy, he still found time to let me and the children know how superior he knew he was.

One day, when we were just beginning addition facts, I presented a problem and one of my quiet little boys, Chris, who seldom volunteered, raised his hand. Of course, I called on him. I was so happy to see that he was paying attention. Chris' answer was wrong.

"He sure is dumb," I heard.

I looked at Robby. "What did you say?"

With a sneer on his face, he repeated, "He sure is dumb," and grinned as he looked around at the other children.

"Oh, no he isn't dumb," I replied. "He just needs help. That's why I am here as a teacher, to help boys and girls learn what they need to know. You know, Robby, we are all different. Does everybody have blue eyes and blond hair like you?"

"No," he answered.

"Look around," I told him. "Some of you have brown eyes, blue eyes, hazel eyes, or green eyes. Some have blond hair, brown hair, black hair or reddish hair. You are different sizes. Some people are tall, some are short, some medium size, some thin and some plump. It's wonderful that we look different so we can tell who is who. I would be confused if I looked around and everybody looked like me. Wouldn't you?"

Robby nodded "Yes."

"Now doesn't it make sense that since we look different on the outside, that we think and learn different on the inside?" I asked as I tapped my temple. "Some people learn faster than others, just like some run faster than others. It doesn't make them any better or any worse, they are just different. They just need help and once they learn, they know as much as anyone else. Doesn't that make sense?"

"Yes," Robby said and I could see, from his expression, that he was thinking it over.

"You happen to be one of the fortunate people who learns very fast, but that does not make you any better than anyone else. There is nothing wrong with Chris. He just needs more help so he will know as much about our addition combinations as you do. Those of us who already know can help those who are learning."

This time, Robby was listening. I had his undivided attention. I continued, "Since you already know how to add numbers, it would be great if you would help Chris with his addition when you have some extra time, after you have finished all of your unsupervised work. Of course, that is up to you, if you want to do it."

Robby looked over at Chris, but he did not say anything.

I continued with my math instruction.

The next day, when there was only five minutes or so before I would finish with a reading group, I saw Robby go over to Chris and start talking to him. He didn't have time to do very much before we had to move on to something else, so he had to go back to his seat.

I went to him and complimented him, "I am pleased to see that you went over to help Chris." Robby smiled.

After a few days, I noticed that Robby seemed to be fussing at Chris and the boy looked as though he was about to cry.

"Robby, go back to your seat, please," I told him.

This time I went over to Robby to explain why I sent him back to his seat. "It is great that you want to help Chris, but you were fussing at him and making him feel bad. Do you see me fussing at the class when I am teaching?"

He shook his head, "No."

"I show them how to do the problems." I smiled at him. "That's the way you can really help him to learn."

A few more days went by and Robby was working hard showing Chris how to add, but Chris was learning very little. Robby was doing all the work.

Again, I spoke to Robby. "I am proud of the way you are showing Chris how to do the problems, but you have to let him do some of the work, too. Show him how to do it then let him do some."

A day or two went by and I could see that the boys seemed to be working together, when all of a sudden, Robby jumped up and excitedly exclaimed, "Mrs. Greenwood, he did it, he did it all by himself!" His eyes were sparkling and Chris was grinning.

"All right, Robby. I'll be there as soon as I finish with reading."

I was elated at the progress that Chris was making; he was slowly learning to do simple addition.

However, I was thrilled most of all with the change in Robby. He was finding so much satisfaction in using his knowledge to help Chris that he was no longer telling me how to run my first grade or criticizing the children in class.

The gym teacher told me that he had changed from the obnoxious, bossy kid he was earlier; now, he tried to help everybody and to do his best.

By Spring, we had him spending more time in the second grade, and Elizabeth informed me that he was well adjusted. Now that his inflated ego had been neutralized, I felt that Robby was ready to move completely into second grade.

I had his mother come for a conference to explain what we had planned. My surprise came when she told me how her son was a different boy at home.

"I can hardly believe how Robby has changed at home," she said. "He used to be a Holy Terror. He would make fun of his little sister, call her stupid and tell her she never did anything right. He would undo everything she did and make her cry. Now, he plays school with her and tries to teach her what he has learned. He helps her do things and makes her happy." I could hardly believe what I was hearing.

She went on, "One day he actually came into the kitchen and asked me if he could help me. I was so surprised, because he always refused to do anything around the house. Now, he sets the table and does whatever he can to help. He talks about you and what you say, all the time."

I was so amazed that I hardly knew what to say. "Thank you for letting me know about the improvement at home. I am proud of Robby and we have developed a great relationship here at school," I assured her. "He is too advanced for my first grade so I have had him working part time in second grade. The second grade teacher and I feel that he is ready to move completely into second grade for the rest of the school year. We wanted you to know."

"You know what is best for Robby, so it will be all right with me," was her reply.

I told Miss Biddick what I wanted to do, but she was a bit concerned about how he would fit into the second grade gym program. We informed the gym teacher that he would be in second grade, and since he was smaller than the other second graders to make sure he could keep up with them.

After three days the report was that Robby was fine - even better than some of the other children in gym.

Later, his mother informed me that Robby wasn't so sure he wanted to be in second grade.

"Why?" I asked in surprise.

"He says he doesn't want to leave Mrs. Greenwood," was the amazing answer.

"Tell Robby that even though he is in second grade, he is still in my register and he can stop by to see me any time," was my reply.

Robby went on to third grade a bright and likable boy.

Many years later Robby wrote to me telling me about his family; the achievements of his grown children and the joyful times he has with his two grandchildren.

The following quote from one of his letters made me feel warm all over:

> "I am still working as a guardian *ad litem* representing abused and neglected children in court.

This kind of work is something that will make you count your blessings. In many cases the problems with the parents are mental illness, drug abuse and alcohol abuse. God bless the grandparents, foster parents and others who take in these kids!"

The joy and satisfaction of helping others that Robby learned in first grade has carried over into his adult life. He is a very caring man.

Education is much more than just academics. It is also the teaching of skills, attitudes and habits that will help children to live satisfying and fulfilling lives.

Summary

Education is the same as building a house. There must be a sound foundation to build on so the structure will last. The beginnings of a strong foundation in education is laid in first grade so that teachers in the following grades can continue to build on it.

First grade is the introduction of formal, scheduled, planned instruction that a child will face the rest of his or her school days. Here's where the preparation for the future begins.

Education is not a lot of "fun and games," it is hard work; **the joy comes in learning**. Parental cooperation is vital in inspiring a child to achieve. Analyzing a child's problem and dealing with it on an individual basis is essential.

"If it ain't broke, don't fix it!" Improve on teaching methods, but do not discard the unchanging factors that work. Continue to teach the following by whatever method it takes: **phonics,** the key that unlocks words; commit to memory **math** combinations that never change - addition, subtraction and later multiplication and division; correct **spelling** at all times; proper **grammar** and legible **penmanship**.

Computers and calculators are essential, but one needs to be able to function when there is no computer or calculator.

Along with basic instruction of reading, math, spelling and penmanship it is important to teach music, art, drama, science, social studies and include games with a bit of fun to create balanced personalities.

Some children will learn more than others, but EVERY CHILD CAN LEARN - SOMETHING!!!

www.ingramcontent.com/pod-product-compliance
Lightning Source LLC
Chambersburg PA
CBHW031521040426
42445CB00009B/344